ROAD GUIDE HALEAKALA AND THE HANA HIGHWAY

Barbara and Robert Decker

Maps and Drawings by Rick Hazlett

Designed by Kristi Carlson

Printed by Dumont Printing
Fresno, California

Published by Double Decker Press
4087 Silver Bar Road
Mariposa, California 95338
© 1992   ISBN: 0-9621019-4-X

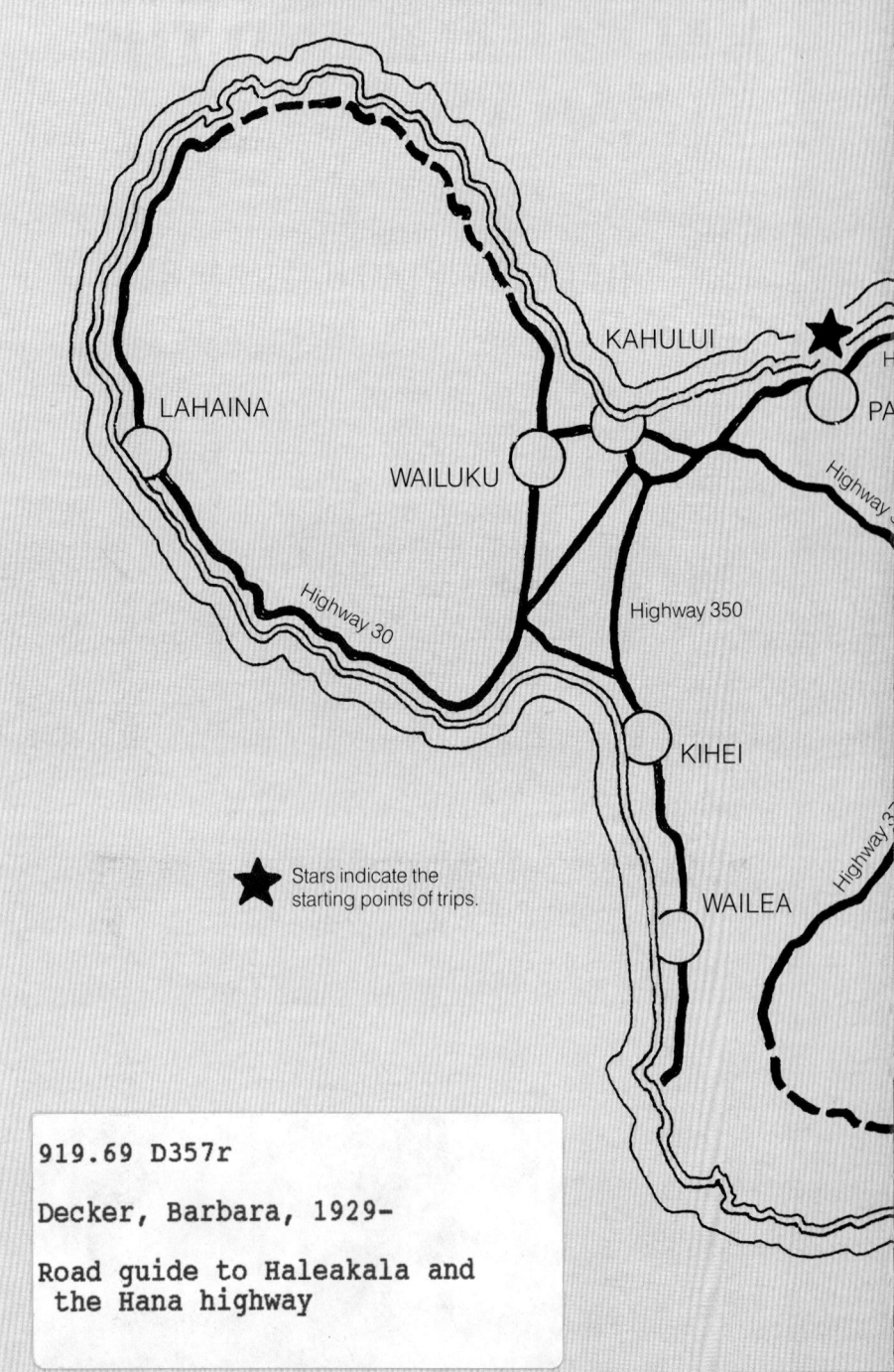

919.69 D357r

Decker, Barbara, 1929-

Road guide to Haleakala and the Hana highway

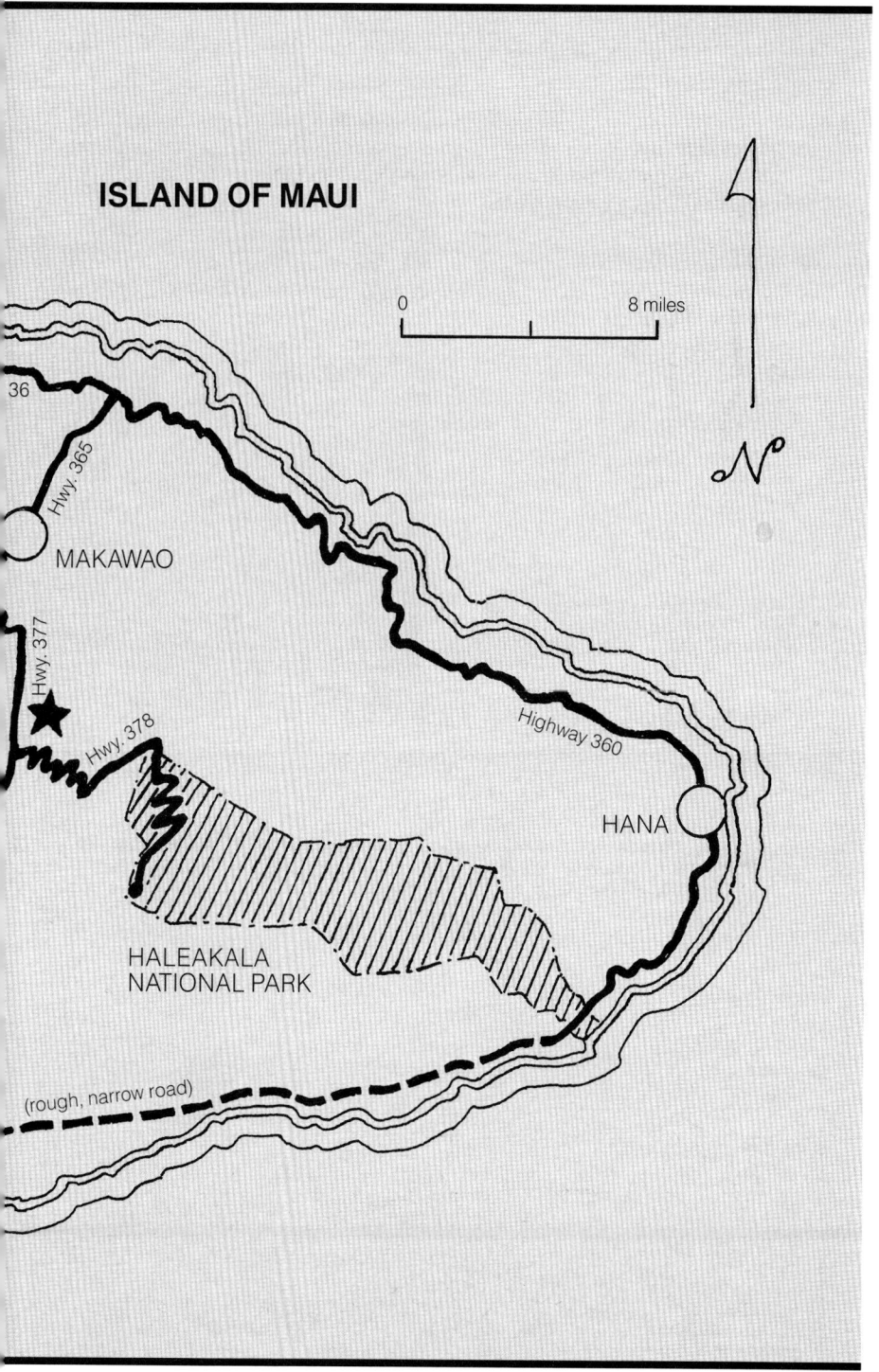

CONTENTS

- 5 **PREFACE**
- 6 **INTRODUCTION**
- 16 **HALEAKALA CRATER ROAD**
- 27 **THE HANA HIGHWAY**
- 43 **HIKING AND CAMPING**
- 47 **SUGGESTED READING**
- 48 **PHOTO CREDITS**

Hapu'u fern

Pincushion protea

PREFACE

Welcome to Haleakala National Park. This book is designed to guide visitors on a driving tour of the major sights in this unique park that encompasses a huge, multihued crater at the top of a towering volcano, and extends down a mysterious, mist-shrouded valley that in less than 8 miles descends from the subalpine zone of the summit to a subtropical rainforest near the ocean. The two parts of the park are not directly connected by road, but the drives to each — both described here — are spectacular additions to the total experience.

This tour is planned for the reader who has about two days for a visit, with the first day a drive to the summit of Haleakala — the House of the Sun — and the second a trip along the famous "Hana Highway" to the Kipahulu section of the National Park. If you are lucky enough to have more time to spend, we strongly suggest that you plan to stay overnight in Hana so you will have a more leisurely drive. If you can stay longer either there or at the summit, you will find several hiking trails listed on page 43. There is no food, lodging or gas available in the park, so carry a picnic and have a full gas tank when you start out.

Besides telling the geologic story of this island volcano, this book also describes something of Haleakala's climate, plants and wildlife. But space is limited and there is much more to be said; for those who have a special interest in any of these topics we include a list of suggested reading with more detailed information.

The starting points for Day 1 and Day 2 are marked on the map on pages 2 and 3. The

Cinder cone

5

following symbols in the text indicate major points of interest:

 Stop in the parking area, climb out of the car and look around.

 Stop in the parking area and take the suggested short walk.

 Things to notice from the car while driving between stops.

The number following the symbol shows the total miles driven. For example, (6.1) means that your mileage indicator should show that it is 6.1 miles since you started your guided tour.

If you are planning to see the sun rise over Haleakala Crater you will have to start very early; the drive from Lahaina or Wailea takes about 2 hours, or 1 1/2 hours from Kahului. Call Park Headquarters for sunrise time and weather information (808 572-7749), and remember that the dawn air at 10,000 feet will be chilly.

INTRODUCTION

Legend says that Haleakala Volcano on the Island of Maui was once the home of Pele, goddess of fire, who is at the heart of Hawai'i's rich mythology. Chased from her volcanic home on Kaua'i by her sister Namakaokaha'i, goddess of the sea, Pele fled first to O'ahu and then to Maui's Haleakala where she lived before moving to Kilauea Volcano on the Big Island.

This story of the odyssey of Pele fits remarkably well with the ages of the Hawaiian island chain as determined by geologists. The lava rocks of Kaua'i are five million years old while those of the Big Island, at the southern end of the chain, are less than one million.

This similarity of myth to the findings of modern science is probably not coincidence. The ancient Hawaiians were excellent observers of their natural world. They must have noticed that the rocks of all the islands are generally the same, and they saw them formed during eruptions of Kilauea and Mauna Loa. They could see that the lava flows of Kaua'i were weathered into deep soils with verdant gardens, and that O'ahu's volcanoes were cut by steep cliffs and canyons. Maui was obviously younger, with Haleakala, its stunningly beautiful volcano, coming to life occasionally in a massive eruption.

The principal Hawaiian chain stretches from the Big Island in the south, northwest across the Pacific to Maui, O'ahu and Kaua'i. But it actually extends far beyond that; past Kaua'i it continues in a northwesterly direction for 2,500 miles with the remnants of eroded, mostly submerged islands of older and older origin. What can account for this strange progression?

Scientists now believe that the Earth's crust is broken into about a dozen plates like a cracked eggshell. These pieces, called plates, are slowly moving in relation to one another. Most volcanoes are found at the edges where the plates pull away or override each other, but occasionally there is a "hot spot" beneath a plate that creates a series of volcanoes as the plate moves slowly over it. Hawai'i, near the middle of the Pacific plate, seems to be over one of

Maui's Two Great Volcanoes

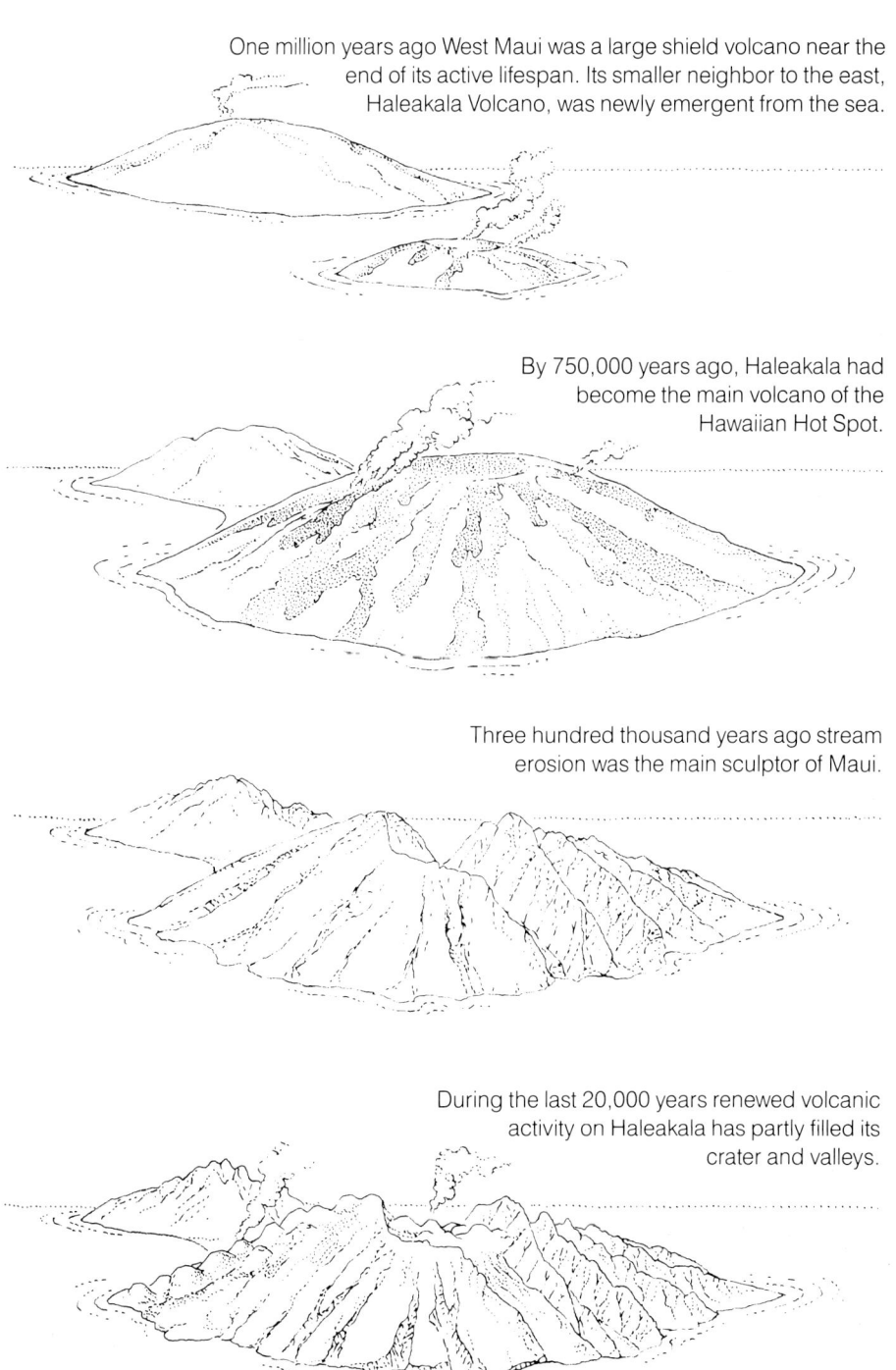

One million years ago West Maui was a large shield volcano near the end of its active lifespan. Its smaller neighbor to the east, Haleakala Volcano, was newly emergent from the sea.

By 750,000 years ago, Haleakala had become the main volcano of the Hawaiian Hot Spot.

Three hundred thousand years ago stream erosion was the main sculptor of Maui.

During the last 20,000 years renewed volcanic activity on Haleakala has partly filled its crater and valleys.

Haleakala sunrise

Kalahaku Pali

these hot spots that generates molten rock. Since the plate is moving over the hot spot at a rate of about four inches a year, the conduit to the surface eventually becomes bent over and shuts off. Then a new conduit forms and another volcano starts building from the deep ocean floor.

Haleakala rises 10,023 feet above its 33-mile diameter base at sea level, and 28,000 feet above its much wider base on the sea floor. Only about 7% of the mass of this gigantic mountain is exposed above the ocean. Its height and its location in the warm, moist trade winds assure the mountain a wealth of diverse climates: warm and rainy as the trades from the northeast strike the coast and rise up the windward slopes, cold and dry above the clouds, and warm and dry on the leeward slopes. These rapidly changing climates encountered as you climb or circle Haleakala by car are delightfully surprising to visitors from more temperate zones.

Hawai'i's unique island ecology is an important part of Haleakala's story. Since Hawai'i is the world's most isolated land mass, all life that arrived on these bare volcanic islands had to come by swimming or floating in the ocean, by flying or drifting through the air, or by hitchhiking in the feathers or digestive tracts of migrating birds. Hawai'i's only two native mammals are a small brown bat and the Hawaiian monk seal; one came by air and the other by sea.

The chance that any living organism could survive the journey and establish itself here was exceedingly remote, but over millions of years a wide variety of plants, insects and birds was able to colonize successfully. Once here, they found few, if any, competitors and an astonishing number of ecological niches to fill in the varied climates and topography of the Hawaiian Islands.

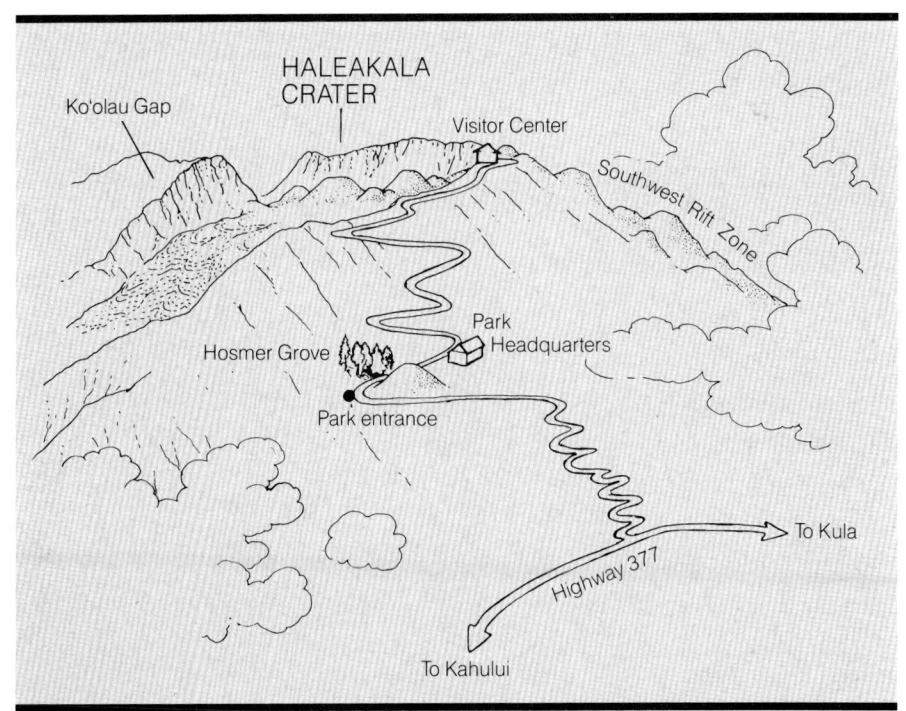

Ka Lua o ka ʻOʻo

Nene

Silversword

Here began one of nature's most remarkable experiments in evolution. Isolated on these remote islands, the new arrivals evolved and diversified rapidly in unexpected and surprising directions, giving Hawai'i an unequaled native flora and fauna.

While plants were becoming established in Hawai'i there were no large animals to graze or browse on them, so as they evolved into specialized forms that could survive in bogs, deserts, jungles and even alpine conditions, they gradually lost most of their defense mechanisms like spines, thorns, and even strong odors. There are Hawaiian mints with almost none of mint's characteristic aroma.

The evolution of Hawai'i's birds, too, has been spectacular. Because of the tremendous distance involved, relatively few land birds found their way to Hawai'i, but they evolved into more than 80 species, one of which produced a whole new family, the Hawaiian honeycreepers. These small, brilliantly colored birds are probably descendants of some sort of finch, but they diversified into more than 45 different species. Some honeycreepers developed very long, curved bills to sip nectar from flowers, some have stout, parrotlike bills to pry away tree bark, and others have straight bills for picking insects from crevices. Birds also had few predators to worry about, so some evolved to be flightless and many others took to building their nests in unprotected places on the ground.

After several million years of very slow colonization, with perhaps only one new life form every 10,000 years, the Hawaiian Islands weren't ready for the one arrival who could really upset the ecological applecart — man. The Polynesians who arrived in about 500 AD brought with them food plants and herbs and some animals such as pigs, dogs and rats. The Polynesian impact was profound; still, the Hawaiian ecosystems probably achieved some balance for the next thousand years until the arrival of Captain Cook and the ships that followed him.

Once Hawai'i's isolation was broken by European contact, dramatic changes came quickly. Cattle, sheep and the extremely destructive goats were introduced and soon became wild. While grazing herds were munching their way through whole forests of defenseless native vegetation, hundreds of species of new plants were being introduced to alter the balance still farther.

Birds too suffered from the onslaught. Their native forest habitats were being destroyed and small predators (rats, cats and mongoose) took a terrible toll on the ground nesting birds, driving some into extinction or near extinction.

More native forests were cleared for ranching. Whole stands of sandalwood trees were lumbered for their highly prized fragrant wood. The result of all this was ecological disaster for Hawai'i's native flora and fauna. One biologist states flatly "There have been more animal and plant species extinguished in the Hawaiian Islands than in all of North America."

It was not until the turn of the century that botanists and biologists began to realize the extent of what was happening and started efforts to slow the trend. The addition of Kipahulu to Haleakala National Park has been one of the most important steps in this direction. By virtue of its remoteness and near-total inaccessibility, this wild, rain shrouded valley has remained almost untouched — a treasurehouse of endangered species.

Drive up to Haleakala Crater and out to Kipahulu. See for yourself the many beautiful faces of this land created by Pele out of fire and rock, and shaped by water, air and time.

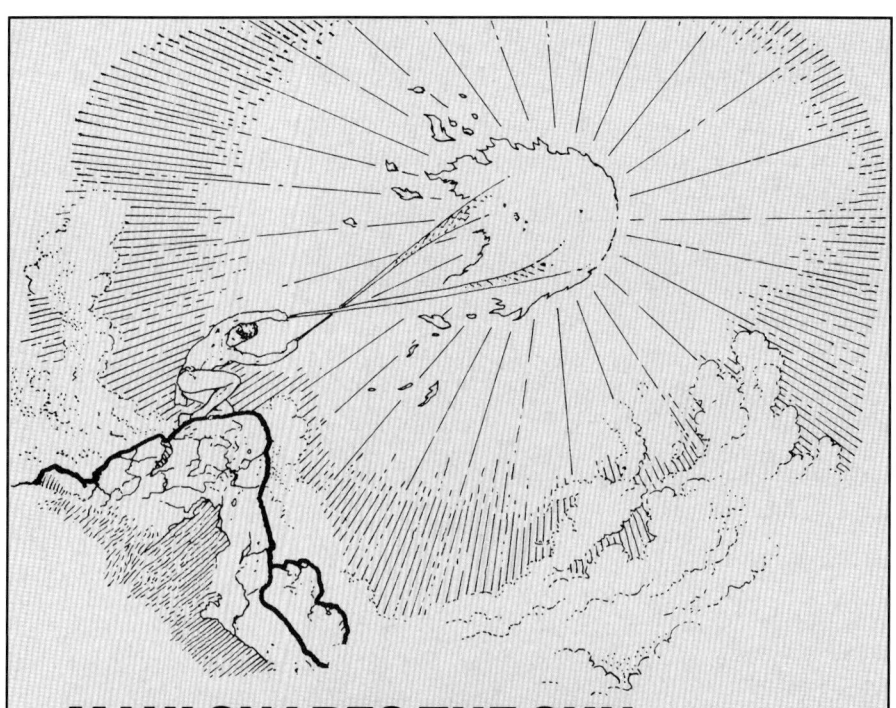

MAUI SNARES THE SUN

In ancient times of legend, the day was only three or four hours long. This was because La, the sun, was so lazy and full of sleep that he would hurry through the sky so he could get back to bed. The whimsical demigod Maui — half man, half god — lived in Hana with his mother Hina, who was a maker of fine tapa cloth. The short hours of sunlight made it hard for Hina to sun-dry her tapa, so the mischievous Maui thought of a plan to lengthen the day. He had noticed that the sun rose over the rim of Haleakala Crater by thrusting first one long sunbeam and then another over the rim, much as a spider would climb over a rock. Using some strong 'ie'ie vines that grow in Hana, Maui wove 16 snares and carried them up Kaupo Gap to Haleakala's summit where he hid in a cave until it was almost time for La to appear. When the first of the sun's legs snaked over the edge, Maui threw a rope around it and made it fast. This he did with each leg in turn, and tied the ropes to a wiliwili tree. La pleaded to be set free, but was in no position to bargain; he had to agree to Maui's demand that he walk slowly and steadily across the sky — a little faster in winter, a little slower in summer — as he has done to this day.

Mamane

Sandalwood

Pilo

Silversword

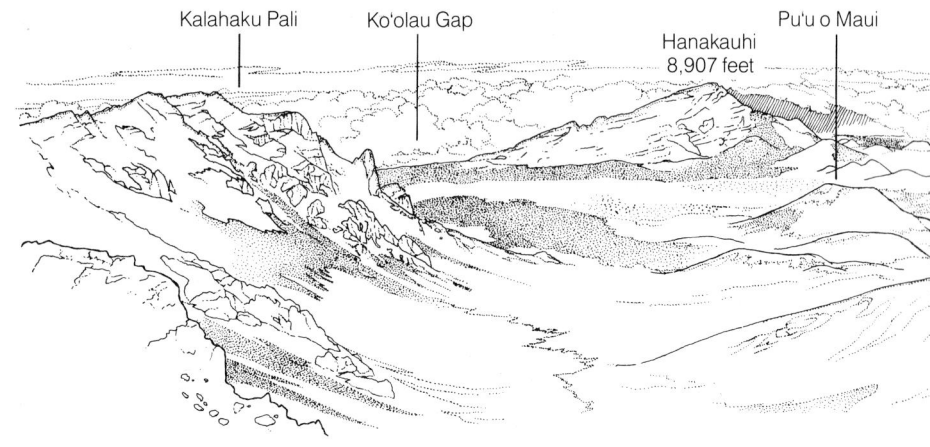

HALEAKALA CRATER ROAD

Time is measured by the dance of the sun and Earth. Haleakala Crater, the House of the Sun, is a special place to pause and think about the great length of geologic time it took to build this world, and the short span of human time that is changing much of it so rapidly.

The Crater Road (Route 378) begins in the upcountry farming and flower-growing district of Kula at an elevation of 3,200 feet. It reaches the summit in 22 miles after 32 switchbacks, climbing an average grade of 6%. As you climb, notice that the temperature is dropping — about 3°F for each 1,000 feet in altitude. If it is 75° near sea level, plan on about 45° at the summit of Haleakala. Set your trip meter to zero at the junction of Routes 377 and 378. The first stop will be in 4.8 miles.

The drive up Haleakala begins among jacarandas, protea and orchid farms, and dark green macadamia nut trees. At (2.1) miles, a cattle guard marks the boundary of the 100-year old Haleakala Ranch, 35,000 acres of grazing land and the setting of Armine von Tempski's autobiography "Born in Paradise". Groves of fragrant eucalyptus trees alternate with rolling grasslands. Clouds circle just overhead or touch down in banks of fog. Rainbows come and go as sun and clouds shift the pot of gold.

Lookout

(4.8) Pull off on the wide, unmarked area to the right side of the road. Ahead out to sea is the uninhabited island of Kaho'olawe. Closer to shore is Molokini, a tiny crescent shaped islet that was formed by an undersea eruption where Haleakala's southwest rift zone extends beneath the ocean. Hot lava exploded violently from contact with shallow seawater and built a

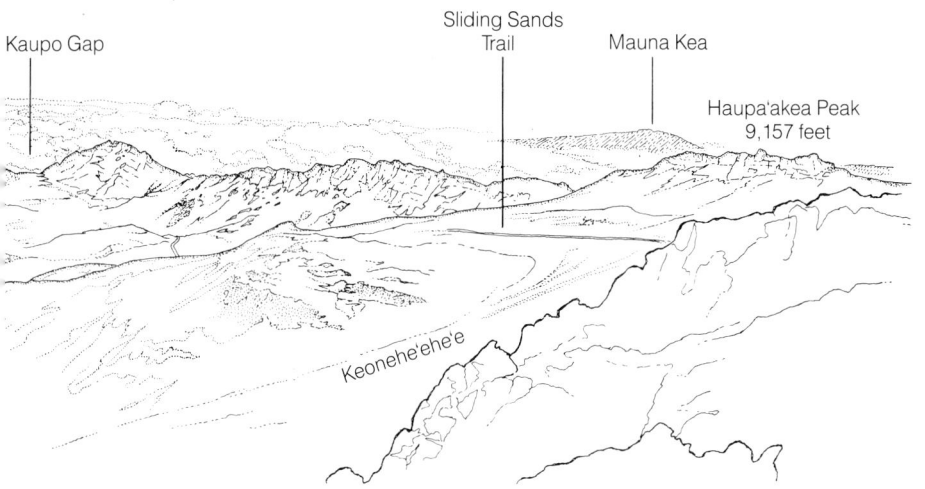

PANORAMA FROM HALEAKALA VISITOR CENTER

typical tuff cone, which has been partially eroded away by waves. If sea levels were to drop, Molokini would be connected to Maui and look much like Diamond Head on O'ahu.

Off to the right is West Maui Volcano, older than Haleakala. The isthmus below, checkerboarded with fields of light green sugarcane and darker green pineapple, connects the two great volcanoes that form Maui. In the distance, partly hidden by West Maui Volcano, is the island of Lana'i. When sea level was 300 feet lower during the ice age 20,000 years ago, Lana'i, Moloka'i, Koho'olawe, and Maui were all connected above sea level into one great island with six volcanoes. See page 7 for a sketch of the evolution of West Maui Volcano and Haleakala.

By this time you have probably seen one or more groups of bicyclists zooming down the mountain. Be wary; some of these riders may not have been on a bike in years. The next stop will be in 6.4 miles.

At (9.5), road cuts on your right provide a look at the inside of a cinder cone. The cinders were sprayed out of a prehistoric volcanic vent as hot, incandescent but solid fragments. They fell around the vent in the inclined layers visible here, building up the cone. Their original black color turned to red as acid gases seeped through the pile of hot cinders, oxidizing the iron-rich compounds in the lava fragments to rusty hues.

After entering Haleakala National Park, notice the turnoff to Hosmer Grove on the left. This will be a stop on the way back down.

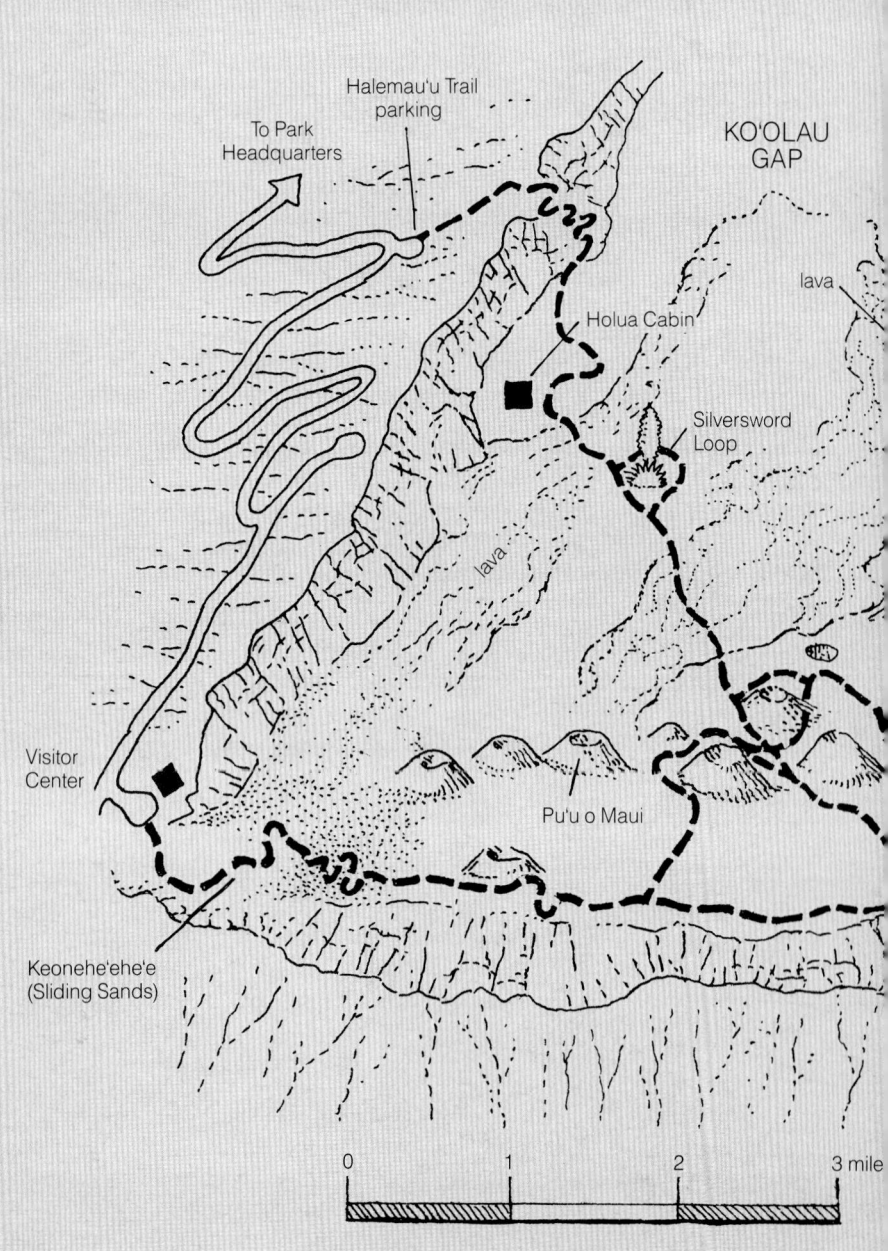

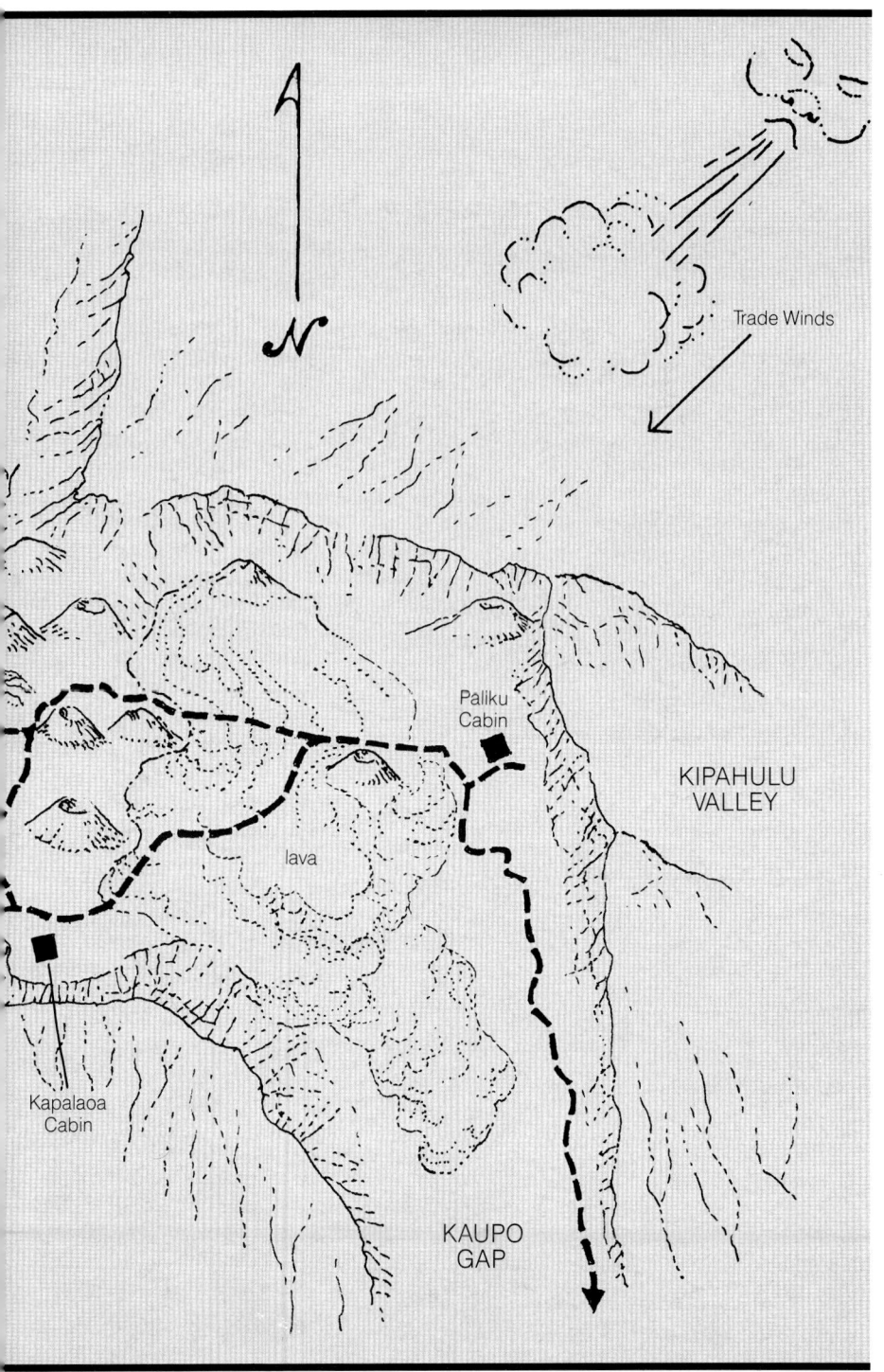

Park Headquarters

(11.2) Stop here to see the exhibits and browse the book display. If you plan to hike into the crater and camp at either of the campgrounds, be sure to get a permit here. Information about reserving the crater cabins for a future trip is also available.

Outside Park Headquarters you might see a nene (Hawaiian goose), the Hawai'i State Bird and a success story in rescue from extinction. Nene apparently evolved from a few Canada geese who were way off course. Once numbered in the tens of thousands, by the 1940s nene were extinct on Maui and by the 1950s down to the last 30 on the Big Island, mostly because of hunting and the introduction of predators like the mongoose. Since that low point, captive breeding and release projects have increased their numbers to a few hundred. The nene is a good example of evolution; instead of swimming in lakes they walk over rough lava flows, so their feet have lost most of their webbing. Maui, Kaua'i and the Big Island are the only places this endangered bird is found in the wild.

Park Headquarters is close to 7,000 feet in elevation — an altitude that generally marks the top of the northeast trade wind clouds. As the trades sweep around this side of Haleakala, eddies sometimes create areas of open sky through the cloud layer as they often do at Pukalani, a town whose name means "hole to heaven". Because of the great variation in temperature and rainfall on Hawai'i's large volcanoes (wet on the windward side, dry to the leeward) many climate zones are crowded close together. On Haleakala you can find tropical humid, tropical desert, temperate, and alpine zones, all within a few miles of each other. In New England there's a saying "If you don't like the weather, just wait 10 minutes." In Hawai'i that could be changed to "If you don't like the weather, just drive 10 miles." The next stop will be in 6.3 miles.

Cloud-filled crater

Perhaps you have noticed how much the vegetation has changed from the Haleakala Ranch to here. The main reasons for this are the higher elevation and the exclusion of cattle from the park. Until the 1920s Haleakala Ranch extended to the summit, and cattle were driven up the steep slopes and into the crater to graze on the grass at Paliku, near the eastern crater wall. Wild goats once foraged and flourished over the high areas of Haleakala, but fencing and hunting have begun to restore much of the park to its more natural state.

From here to the summit the vegetation is subalpine shrubland consisting largely of mamane trees, with clusters of bright yellow blossoms; bushes of pukiawe, with needle like foliage and pink-white berries; pilo, with orange berries; and 'ohelo, with juicy red edible berries.

At (14.8) miles the parking lot near a switchback is the start of the Halemau'u Trail into Haleakala Crater. From the road to the rim of the crater by this trail is about one mile, and another 3 miles to the crater floor.

Leleiwi Overlook

(17.5) Pull into the parking lot on the right, cross the road on foot and take the short, 200-yard trail to the overlook for a panoramic view of the vast crater of Haleakala. This huge depression is 7.5 miles long (east west), 2.5 miles wide, and 3,000 feet deep. Manhattan Island could fit inside, and you would look down on the tops of the skyscrapers. The view is often described as a moonscape; the barren rocks and volcanic shapes do capture that image. But the colors — muted shades of purple, gray, rust and yellow — add great beauty to the scene, and the sunlight and swirling clouds keep changing the hues and patterns.

Sometimes in late afternoon clouds bank up inside the crater and block the view from here. If this occurs and the sun is behind you, look into the cloudy mist directly away from the sun. You may be lucky enough to see what Hawaiians called the Ho'okuaka, and Europeans call the Specter of the Brocken. Around your shadow in the mist will be a halo of colors. This same phenomenon can sometimes be seen from an airplane window if you are looking down on a cloud top; the shadow of the plane is encircled by an apparent rainbow. However, the specter is not a true rainbow — the curvature is tighter. It is caused by the small spaces between the cloud droplets (diffraction) rather than by the bending of light rays within the droplets that forms a rainbow (refraction). Physics or metaphysics — nature is mysterious and miraculous. The next stop will be in 3.8 miles.

Notice how the vegetation has changed from near Park Headquarters at the 7,000 foot elevation, where there were mostly low bushes with a few outcrops of lava. Here at 9,000 feet the landscape is mostly exposed lava and cinders with scant vegetation. The low temperatures (it sometimes snows here), wind, thin air, and the sun's ultraviolet rays conspire to make life difficult at high elevations. At (20.7) miles turn right to the summit instead of entering the Visitor Center parking lot straight ahead; this will be a stop on the way back down.

21

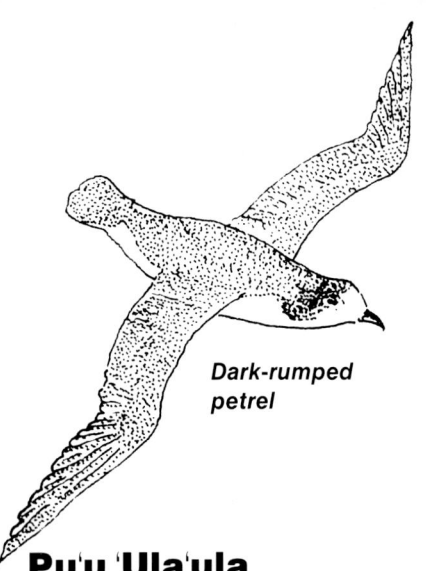

Dark-rumped petrel

Pu'u 'Ula'ula

(21.3) This cinder cone called Pu'u 'Ula'ula (Red Hill), on the west rim of the crater, is the highest point on Haleakala. Climb the steps to the shelter or take the more gradual ramp from the far end of the parking lot. Looking southeast to the Big Island you can probably see the high summits of Mauna Loa and Mauna Kea Volcanoes, each over 13,000 feet in elevation.

Haleakala's summit elevation is 10,023 feet, but the mountain was once much higher than this. Hawaiian volcanoes gradually sink because their great weight slowly bends down the Earth's crust beneath them. Maui now appears to be stable, but the Big Island is still sinking at a rate of one tenth inch per year. That doesn't sound like much, but in half a million years it adds up to more than 4,000 feet. In addition, the summits of Hawaiian volcanoes often collapse into large, steep-walled basins called calderas a few miles wide and as much as a thousand feet deep. Erosion has carved out so much of the summit crater of Haleakala that it is difficult to know how much, if any, of the present basin formed by collapse. By analogy to the Big Island's Mauna Loa and Kilauea, active volcanoes with major summit calderas, probably some of the old high summit of Haleakala was lowered by caldera collapse. Taking into account slow island subsidence, rapid caldera collapse, and thousands of years of erosion, it can be inferred that the once lofty summit of Haleakala — a mile or so east of Pu'u 'Ula'ula — probably reached an elevation of 13,000 to 14,000 feet.

About 500 yards to the southwest, just outside the park on the next cinder cone of the rift, is Science City. (A rift is a zone of weakness on a volcano along which eruptions tend to occur. The southwest rift of Haleakala, marked by a line of cinder cones, extends from the summit for 14 miles to the sea with Molokini its farthest visible cone.) Science City, a cluster of high-altitude observatories, tracks satellites, measures the wobble of the moon, and conducts other space research. Measurements made here have confirmed the theory of plate tectonics; the Pacific Plate, with Maui onboard, does move about 4 inches northwestward every year.

The summit parking lot is built in the shallow crater of Pu'u 'Ula'ula. Where the ramp meets the parking lot there are some large volcanic bombs — pieces of once-molten lava that were hurled from the vent and hardened as they whirled through the air. The largest bomb is about 4 to 5 feet across.

The summit of Haleakala is the altar of the sunrise. It is freezing cold here at dawn, and sunrise watchers from beach resorts huddle in hotel bedspreads and tablecloths, hoping the sun will speed up, not slow down. Sunsets are equally beautiful and much warmer. Check a newspaper or call Park Headquarters (752-7749) for sunrise or sunset time, and plan an hour's drive from the Crater Road intersection to reach here.

Start down the hill again; the next stop will be in 0.6 mile.

House of the Sun Visitor Center

(21.9) Turn right at the intersection into the large parking lot. The crater view from the Visitor Center is Haleakala's best (see panorama on pages 16-17).

How did this vast crater come to be? Molten rock, earthquakes, rain, gravity, ice, and wind have all played their part, but like any masterpiece it took time — in this case about a million years. Haleakala's youth is gone but it is reasonable to guess that it grew like its neighbor volcanoes on the Big Island, though a generation earlier. Seven hundred thousand years ago Haleakala probably looked much like Mauna Loa does today, a large dome-like mountain with gently sloping sides. Then its fires diminished and erosion, particularly stream erosion in the early valleys of Ke'anae and Kaupo, began to cut deep canyons into Haleakala's flanks. The heads of those two deep canyons, Ke'anae (Ko'olau Gap) on the north and Kaupo on the south, almost merged near the volcano's summit and carved out the crater to depths even greater than you see today.

All this took some tens to hundreds of thousands of years; no one really knows how long. What is known is that this period of erosion cut deep valleys into a series of older lava flows. Then the resulting canyons and enlarged crater were partly filled by younger flows. Both groups of flows have been dated by radioactivity techniques, and the major period of

VOLCANO FACTS

Name: Haleakala

Type of volcano: shield volcano (gentle, dome-shaped profile; convex upward)

General composition: basaltic

Ancient maximum height: 13,000 to 14,000 feet

Present height: 10,023 feet

Oldest exposed lavas: 750,000 years old in Honomanu Valley

Youngest exposed lavas: 1790 AD eruption at 1200-foot elevation on southwest rift zone; flows extend 3 miles southwest into the sea

Major period of eruption: 1,250,000 to 750,000 years ago

Size of crater: 7.5 miles long (east-west), 2.5 miles wide, 3,000 feet deep

Age of crater: formed mainly by erosion between 400,000 and 20,000 years ago

Coldest recorded temperature at summit: 12°F

Warmest recorded temperature at summit: 73°F

23

Snow above 9,000 feet

erosion is bracketed by their ages — early flows 400,000 or more years ago; later flows 10,000 or fewer years ago.

There is no precise historical record of Haleakala's most recent eruption, but an interesting piece of detective work places it at about 1790. It seems that when the explorer La Perouse mapped Maui's shoreline in 1786 he showed a broad, shallow bay between two points on the southwest coast. A few years later Vancouver charted the same area; his map made in 1793 showed a prominent peninsula between those points. Combined with the fact that the peninsula lava flow looks very young, and that local legend tells of eruptions at approximately that time, 1790 seems like a reasonable date. The area south of the flow is now known as La Perouse Bay. A few cinder cones in the crater and along the east rift to Hana are less than 1,000 years old.

Haleakala Crater has been touted as "the world's largest extinct crater", a quote that makes geologists flinch. It is almost surely not extinct, but only dormant. True volcanic craters form by explosion or collapse, not by erosion; and Lake Toba in Indonesia lies in a much larger crater (caldera) — 60 miles long. Nevertheless, Haleakala Crater is a wondrous, beautiful place, as is fitting for the House of the Sun.

Pull on stout shoes and a jacket and hike part way down the Sliding Sands Trail from the south side of the parking lot just past White Hill (see map on page 18). Descending two or three switchbacks (about a half mile) is enough to give you a feeling of the vastness and silence of the crater. The sliding sands are volcanic ash and cinders that have partly filled this end of the crater. At this altitude it takes about twice as long to hike back up the trail as it did to walk down.

The next stop is in 2.3 miles. When driving down the mountain remember to use a lower gear. Brakes can fail from overheating.

Kalahaku Overlook

(24.2) Turn right at (23.9) miles on a short road to the parking area. The rim overlook at 9,324 feet provides another spectacular view of the crater floor dotted with cinder cones that range in color from gray to orange to red. From this distance the cinder cones seem small, but they vary in height up to 600 feet. Sharp eyes may pick out a hiker on the thread-like trails below; only then can the vast scale of the crater be appreciated.

The cinder cones and crater-floor flows are considered to be geologically young, though charcoal samples for radiocarbon dating have not been found within Haleakala Crater. About 20 eruptions are thought to have taken place within the crater during the past 2,500 years. This estimate is based on the observation that many lava flows of various ages within the crater are not covered by a red ash deposit thought to have fallen about 2,500 years ago that is found in other parts of the summit area. Another less scientific clue to the ages of volcanic features in Hawai'i is the use of the name Pele in Hawaiian place names. For example, Pu'u o Pele (Hill of Pele) is a cinder cone on the south floor of Haleakala Crater. A place name that includes Pele often implies that volcanic activity was witnessed there by ancient Hawaiians, thus it probably occurred sometime after the 500 AD arrival of Polynesians to Hawai'i.

Downslope from the Kalahaku parking lot is an area covered with many silverswords. This unusual plant, unique to Haleakala, is a marvel of adaptation. A relative of the sunflower, it has evolved to withstand the punishing extremes of climate at these altitudes. Seen at a distance, a silversword is a shimmering sphere the color of moonlight. The Hawaiians called it 'ahinahina, the word for gray repeated twice. Up close, it is a rosette as much as 2 feet across with slim, sword-shaped leaves covered with a lustrous silvery down. The bloom stalk is spectacular (page 11), often several feet tall with a hundred or more purple flowers. Silverswords live from 15 to more than 50 years, bloom once and die.

Early explorers described the cinder cones in Haleakala Crater as being covered with so many silverswords they looked like snowdrifts, but by the 1920s these plants were almost extinct. The main culprits were the wild goats that ate almost everything in sight. People were a close second, though; souvenir hunters or hikers who would roll the shining globes downhill almost completed the destruction. The creation of Haleakala National Park saved the silversword. Protection and the work of dedicated botanists have brought them back from a low of barely 100 plants in 1927 to more than 40,000 today. Even so, the silversword and other native species may be threatened by ongoing changes in the ecology of Maui. The silversword is pollinated by native bees, moths and flies. Invaders like yellowjackets and the Argentine ant may eventually threaten the survival of these native insects. The next stop will in 9.2 miles, below Park Headquarters.

At (32.9) miles turn right to Hosmer Grove. In 0.2 mile there is a drainage dip in the road and about 100 feet beyond the dip, on the right, is a beautiful sandalwood tree. Sandalwood was precious in China for incense and aromatic wood carvings, and the Pacific sailing-ship trade in the 1800s nearly destroyed the Hawaiian sandalwood forests.

Hosmer Grove

(33.4) A half-mile-long nature trail winds through this misty, dark forest of introduced trees. In 1910 Ralph Hosmer planted this and other groves of trees like eucalyptus from Australia, sugi pine from Japan, deodar from India, Douglas fir and several species of pine from mainland United States, along with other species as an experiment in establishing a timber industry as well as helping to reestablish the watershed. A unique botanical grove with historical significance, it presents the dilemma of the struggle between native plants and introduced species. The Park Service, whose goals include preservation of Haleakala's native plants and animals, keeps these non-native trees from escaping into the wild and encourages the regrowth of native plants on the surrounding slopes.

At the start of the trail pick up the brochure that describes both the introduced trees and several native trees and shrubs at numbered markers along the walk. The dense aromatic forest of introduced trees along the first half of the trail contrasts sharply with the smaller trees of the more open native plant community.

This is the last stop on today's tour. Tomorrow's drive along the Hana Highway to the Kipahulu section of the Park begins at Lower Pa'ia (see map on next page).

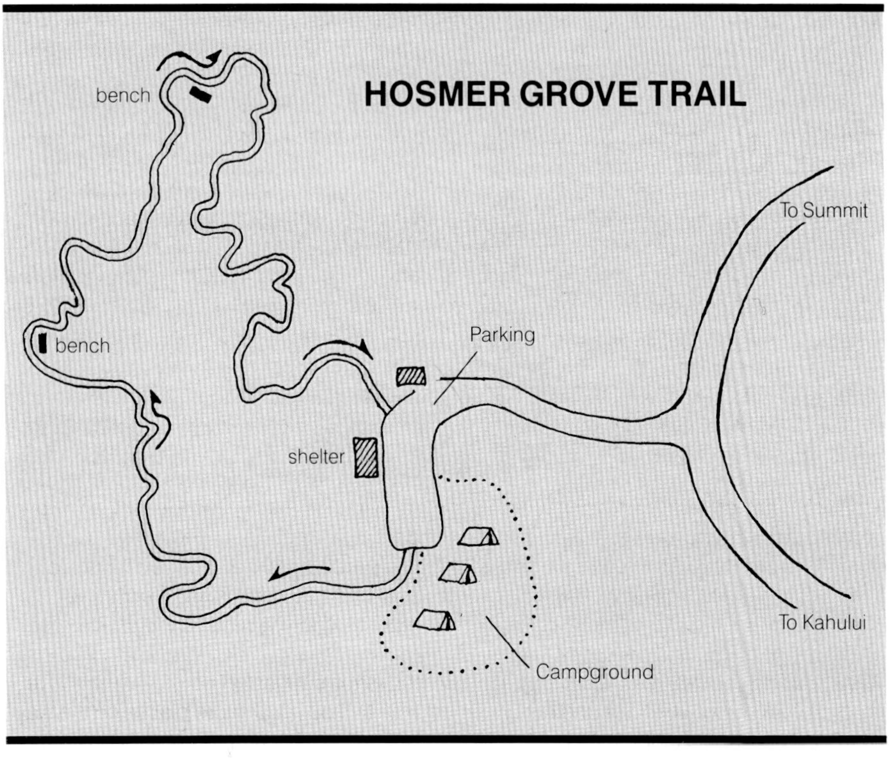

HOSMER GROVE TRAIL

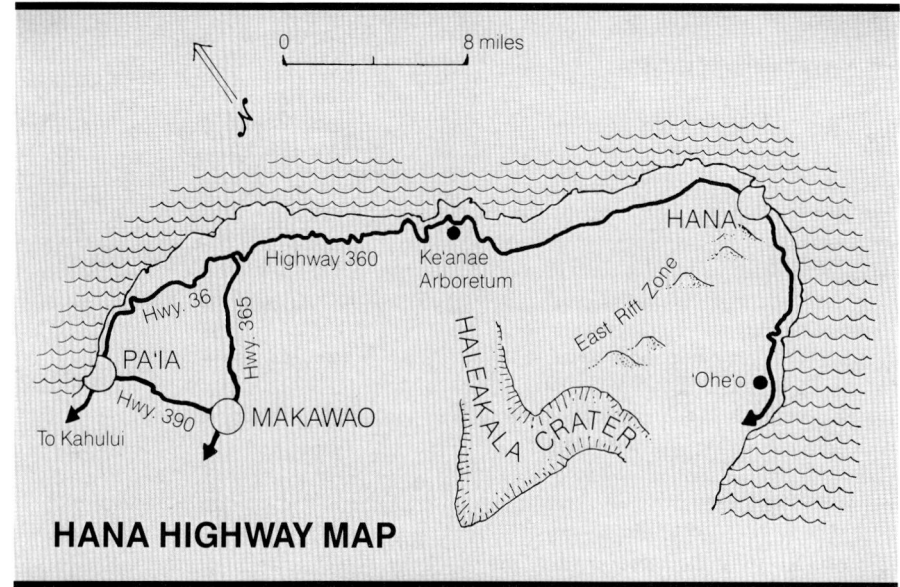

THE HANA HIGHWAY

The second day's trip includes a drive along the infamous Hana Highway as it hairpins its way through one of Hawai'i's most beautiful tropical rainforests, and a visit to the Kipahulu section of Haleakala National Park where 'Ohe'o Stream cascades down through pools and waterfalls to meet the ocean. Kipahulu Valley stretches from the 7,000 foot rim of Haleakala Crater to the shoreline. The tranquil beauty of the pools gives little hint of the wild, forested canyons just a few miles upstream, where more than 250 inches of rain falls every year.

Above 2,000 feet, Kipahulu Valley is an almost impenetrable jungle of moss-bearded 'ohi'a and koa trees, and a tangle of ferns, tree ferns and vines. Bounded by sheer cliffs, some reaching 1,500 feet in height and with countless waterfalls and cascades, upper Kipahulu is constantly shrouded in fog and rain which only add to its ethereal beauty. This remote valley is a haven, and in some cases a last refuge, for many of Hawai'i's endangered species of plants and birds — most of which, as products of Hawai'i's unique island ecology, live nowhere else on Earth. The upper valley has been designated a Scientific Research Reserve and is open only to qualified scientists, but the lower valley, the scenic threshold to this rich wilderness, is open for all to see and enjoy.

This will be a long day so try to get an early start. The mileages are not too long — the roundtrip from Kahului is 126 miles and 175 miles from Lahaina, but the road is slow and the scenery seductive. You will see probably 100 places you'll want to stop and each one is worthwhile; we recommend you resist, though, if you are making the trip in one day, and make just the stops suggested here. You may have time to stop a few more places on the way back. If you have an extra day consider staying overnight in Hana, but be sure to make a reservation in advance or take camping gear.

All day you will be traveling on the flanks of giant Haleakala Volcano, but the scenery is totally different than that at the summit. Dense tropical foliage, deep stream canyons, waterfalls, and narrow one-lane bridges (54 or 56, depending on who is counting) over steep fern-filled gullies, and precipitous cliffs where white foam meets black lava are just some of the visual treats along the way.

The mileage log starts at Lower Pa'ia (see map on page 27). Set your odometer to zero in the center of town where Baldwin Avenue meets Route 36. Don't try to use the highway mileposts; they stop and start several times.

Pa'ia is an old plantation mill town that has been partly restored with new shops and restaurants. The Pa'ia Sugar Mill is just above town, but the workers no longer live in the camps that once ringed the town and housed 10,000 laborers. This is a good place to buy picnic supplies for the trip and to fill your gas tank; there are no stores or gas stations between Pa'ia and Hana. The first stop will be in 2.2 miles.

Ho'okipa State Park

(2.2) This beach park has a sheltered tidal pool where children can play. The real attraction here, though, are the world class waves that roll in across the Pacific. International competitions in surfing and, more recently, windsurfing are held here. Unless the weather is truly awful you should see a flock of bright colored sailboards skipping over and through the wild waves. The best view is from the first (highest) parking area above the beach. The next stop will be in 18.7 miles.

When you leave Ho'okipa you are still traveling through lush sugar cane fields that reach almost to the ocean. Sugar is one of Maui's major industries, though it has been declining in recent years. Most of the fields between here and Kahului are irrigated by water from an extensive system of many miles of ditches and tunnels, built in the late 19th and early 20th centuries to carry water from the rain drenched north slope of Haleakala to sunny central Maui.

At (4.2) look upslope for a view of Haleakala's north rift unless it is obscured by low clouds. The prominent hills are cinder cones that mark prehistoric eruption sites on this side of Haleakala. The north rift has not been volcanically active for the past 20,000 years.

By (4.5) miles the sugar cane has given way to pineapple fields — another of Maui's important crops. If it is picking season, notice how the workers are swathed in heavy clothes to protect themselves from the sharp, jagged leaves. In the next few miles you'll see banana trees, coconut palms, mango trees shaped like huge hot-air balloons — just a hint of the tropical foliage to come. Even on this undeveloped coast, though, most of the brightly flowering ornamentals like poinciana, African tulip tree, plumeria and bougainvillea are not native but introduced species.

Near (12) miles you will start to see whole hillsides and roadcuts covered with tangled masses of light green ferns. This is uluhe, or false staghorn fern, a Hawai'i native (see background photo on pages 34-35). Its intertwined stems make hiking across slopes like these almost impossible.

The neat little settlement of Kailua at (15.6) miles is headquarters for the East Maui Irrigation Company, responsible for tending the long ditch system that you will see in several places along the road.

By (16.2) miles the road is snaking through dense forests of bamboo, often carpeted with impenetrable mats of uluhe. When you see these forests and the deep gulches yet to come, it is easy to understand why early Hawaiians would traverse the island by climbing up Haleakala, crossing the barren crater and dropping down the other side.

The forest around (17.3) miles is a superb example of tropical rainforest with an inseparable profusion of native and non-native trees, palms, ferns and vines. One large tree that is easy to identify is the kukui, with conspicuously pale green leaves. Look for patches of them on hillsides and in gulches. The small trees with fruit that looks like lemons are guava, a vigorous invader from South America.

Narrow one-lane bridges are common in this part of the Hana Highway. Look upstream every time you cross one and you'll probably be rewarded with a view of another rushing waterfall. Near the bridge at (18.5) miles you can see some of the irrigation diversion works.

At (19.4) miles is the Waikamoi Ridge Nature Trail, a beautiful path through a damp forest of eucalyptus, ginger, paperbark, heliconia, and much more, all laced together with giant philodendron vines. This trail is described on page 46; plan to stop on your return trip if you are early enough, or have a walk now if you are spending an extra day.

Puohokamoa Falls

(20.9) Pull off and park in the small parking area just before the bridge. A short walk — less than 1/4 mile — through a tunnel of vines, ferns, ginger and ti plants leads to a beautiful double waterfall and pool on Puohokamoa stream. Most waterfall pools like this one are safe for a swim unless the streams are really raging or you see a "No Swimming" sign. Don't be tempted to drink the water, though — giardia is always a possibility. The next stop will be in 1.2 miles.

Kaumahina State Wayside

(22.1) This delightful small park affords a wonderful view of the ocean, the dramatic coast line and Ke'anae Peninsula in the background. The peninsula was formed by a prehistoric but geologically young lava flow that streamed down Ke'anae Valley from the crater of Haleakala to the sea. The park is bright with lots of tropical flowers (some with name tags) shaded by eucalyptus and paperbark. There are restrooms and picnic tables here, too. The next stop will be in 4.4 miles.

This section of the Hana Highway offers spectacular views of the ocean as the road clings to steep cliffs and dips in and out of deeply indented ravines. Ahead at (22.5) miles is a hillside of weirdly shaped trees; these are hala (pandanus), with aerial prop roots and spiky leaves, and fruit that looks like pineapple. Other tropical trees crowd the roadway; if you're driving in a convertible watch out for dropping guavas.

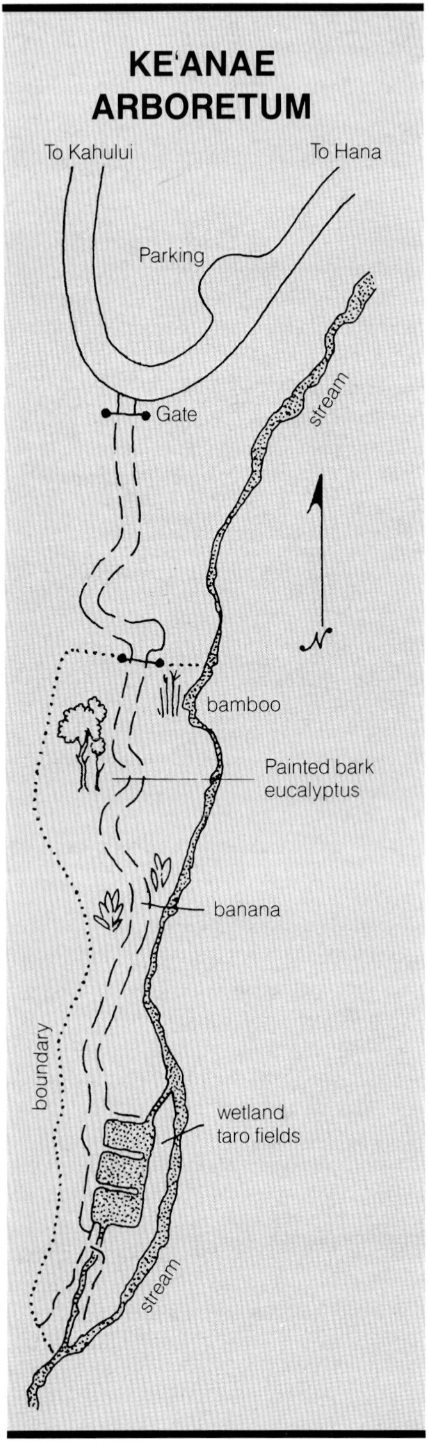

KE'ANAE ARBORETUM

To Kahului
To Hana
Parking
Gate
stream
N
bamboo
Painted bark eucalyptus
banana
boundary
wetland taro fields
stream

Ke'anae Botanical Garden

(26.5) Stop in a parking area shaded by immense monkeypod trees. The arboretum covers 6 acres with trees, flowers and food plants growing in lavish profusion. An almost-level path, about 3/4 mile round trip, leads through banks of colorful impatiens, huge "elephant ears" called 'ape (ah-pay), and the main section of the gardens. Most plants have name markers. There is a grove of palms both native and introduced, all varieties of ginger — torch, red, white, Kahili, and more — heliconias, plumerias and countless other ornamentals.

Notice the brilliant colors of the painted bark eucalyptus, one of the few eucalyptus not native to Australia but to the Philippines instead. A pathway lined with large ti plants leads to a native planting section with taro patches between lava rock walls. Here also are several varieties of bananas, some heavy with fruit, as well as papayas and towering breadfruit trees. Wander some of the meanders of the paths on your way back, but try not to spend more than about half an hour. The next stop will be in 0.4 mile.

Ke'anae Overlook

(26.9) At (26.6) miles a road on the left leads down to the Ke'anae Peninsula; it is a delightful side trip if you have more than a day for Hana and Kipahulu. If not, pull into the next overlook on your left and admire the neat geometric taro patches and groves of bananas and coconuts below. Rice used to be grown here by Chinese who came originally as cane field workers. The next stop will be in 1.9 miles.

Breadfruit leaves

Wailua Valley Lookout

 **(28.8)** Stop in the parking area on the right side of the road. Just for a change, this is a view away from the ocean with sweeping views up the wide valley. If clouds aren't too low, you can see all the way to the Ko'olau Gap of Haleakala Crater's rim. After erosion enlarged the crater some 100,000 years ago, Ke'anae Valley was much deeper than you see it today. Renewed eruptions in the crater during the past 10,000 years have sent many streams of lava out through Ko'olau and down to the sea, filling the once-deep canyon with a thick floor of younger flows. The most recent flow, not yet dated, forms the flat Ke'anae Peninsula. The probability of future lava flows coursing down Ke'anae Valley is estimated by geologists to be about one flow every 2,000 years.

Walk up the steps through a tunnel of tangled hau branches; hau is a native tree, a member of the hibiscus family. Its bright yellow flowers open every morning, turning to a deep orange by late afternoon. The village down by the ocean is Wailua. The next stop will be in 3.8 miles.

 For the next few miles after you leave Wailua there is a new, beautiful waterfall around almost every bend in the road. Waikane, at (29.5) miles, is one of the best. At (32) miles the irrigation ditch runs right beside the road.

MAUI PULLS UP THE ISLANDS

Near 'Alau Island, just offshore from Hana, the mischievous demigod Maui put to sea on his most important mission. With his magic fishhook, he was going to pull up a great land mass from the bottom of the ocean. Maui pushed off in his canoe, and paddled until he was in the open sea. He took out his magic fishhook, and to increase its sacred power he used for bait the 'alae, or mudhen, that was revered in its own right as a benefactor for bringing fire to the people of old and wore red feathers the color of fire on its head. At the last minute the 'alae warned Maui "When you feel something on your hook, paddle hard and don't look back."

Maui swung the baited hook over his head in ever-increasing circles until his rope was almost played out, and then let it fly. It sailed in a mighty arc and hit the ocean with a tremendous splash. He started paddling as the hook sank to the bottom, and was soon aware that something huge had been caught. As he paddled harder and harder, he could feel the gigantic mass rising behind him. Fearful that it would slip off his hook he decided to secure it with his net, but when he turned back and threw the net the land shattered into many pieces. The pieces are still in the sea, known today as the Hawaiian Islands. His magic hook is seen in the sky as the star group Maui's Fishhook; those unfamiliar with Maui call it the constellation Scorpius.

Hamoa Beach

Pua'a Ka'a State Park

(32.6) Pua'a Ka'a is another good place to stop and take a short walk through a garden of tropical plants, pools and lawns with picnic tables. There are restrooms here too. The pools under the fern-banked waterfalls are safe for a cool swim. The name Pua'a Ka'a translated means "rolling pig", though you're not apt to see one. Hana is 12.4 miles ahead.

After leaving Pua'a Ka'a the road stays at almost 1,000 feet above the ocean for several miles. At (35) miles a road to the left leads to Nahiku, a small village with an abandoned wharf. Around the turn of the century a large rubber plantation was started here and several experimental varieties of rubber trees were planted. However, at Nahiku the average yearly rainfall is 150 inches, and upslope from the highway it exceeds 350 inches. The high rainfall hampered the trees' growth and difficulties in shipping made the venture uneconomical; in spite of the high hopes of the developers the industry was abandoned after about ten years.

At (41) miles a road to the left leads to the Hana Airport, the quick way to get back and forth to the outside world. Notice now how the landscape is opening up as the road nears Hana, with the deep forests giving way to cultivated fields and pasture land. At (42) miles a road to the left leads to Wai'anapanapa State Park, a fascinating place to spend a few hours. If you have some extra time, explore the picturesque coast, Wai'anapanapa Caves and fresh water pools. This area is rich in history, with many ancient Hawaiian house platforms, gravesites, and a double heiau (temple).

At (45) miles the road reaches Hana, the town that gives the road its name. For nearly a century Hana was a big sugar producing area with thousands of workers from China, Japan, the Philippines and Portugal. The hilly terrain made mechanization difficult, though, and by World War II the sugar industry here was just about finished. Ranching became the mainstay, and population dropped to around 1,000. Today most of the locals, many of whom are of Hawaiian descent, work for the Hotel Hana Maui or for Hana Ranch. Explore the town if you have an extra day; there is a small museum, but most of the visual delights are outdoors.

Hana Bay is guarded by the cinder cone Ka'uiki, the hill fortress of Hawaiian chiefs, that marks the end of Haleakala's east rift zone on land. The rift zone continues for many miles under the sea. Near Ka'uiki, Hawaiian Queen Ka'ahumanu, wife of King Kamehameha, was born in 1768. This is a good spot for a swim and a picnic.

By this time few odometers will register the same mileage traveled, so reset your trip meter to zero at the Hotel Hana Maui (right on the highway) before driving on to Kipahulu. The next stop will be in 2.9 miles.

At the far end of town, (0.4) mile, is the site of the famous Hasegawa General Store, which unfortunately burned down in 1990. Plans are afoot to rebuild, so you may have a chance to see a new version of this store that has always been a happy conglomeration of almost anything one would want to buy.

As you drive through the pasturelands beyond Hana, look upslope to see a row of cinder cones, Haleakala's east rift zone. Although most of the eruption vents on the east rift have not been dated, some are probably only a few hundred years old. A lava flow in Kawaipapa Gulch, just upstream from Hana, has charcoal beneath it with a radiocarbon age of 500 years.

At (1.8) miles turn left on Haneo'o Road, near the cinder cone called Ka Iwi o Pele (The Bones of Pele). Just past the intersection is a small beach park called Koki; it was here that the legendary demigod Maui performed his famous feat of pulling the Hawaiian Islands up from the bottom of the sea (see page 32). Offshore is a little remnant island called 'Alau, now a seabird sanctuary.

Hamoa Bay

(2.9) At Hamoa Bay, the second beach park on Haneo'o Road, find a parking space and walk to the beach down a short trail that is lush with spider lilies, plumeria and hala. This is probably the best swimming spot on this side of Maui; a beautiful curving beach rimmed with coconut trees. The beach chairs and umbrellas are for the use of Hotel Hana Maui guests, but the beach is open to everyone. The next stop will be in 4.9 miles.

🚗 The coast road rejoins the main road at (3.4) miles, and beyond this point it becomes even rougher and narrower than before. On both sides of the road are homes — some lavish and some modest, but almost all with a profusion of beautiful tropical plants in well-tended yards. Beyond the pastures of the Hana Ranch the tropical jungle takes over again; at (6.5) miles you are driving beneath an archway of huge mango trees. In mango season the road will probably be covered with fragrant fruit. Waterfalls, like the one at (7.5) miles, crash down right beside the road.

Wailua Falls

🚗 **(7.8)** Wailua Falls probably lives up to everyone's vision of what a tropical waterfall should look like. Filmy waters drift down almost 100 feet to a clear pool below, fringed with ferns, ginger and vines. Photographing these falls through a branch of dark green, deeply serrated breadfruit leaves is almost impossible to resist. The next stop will be in 2.8 miles.

🚗 At (10.4) the road reaches 'Ohe'o Bridge, just inside Haleakala National Park. This area used to be known as Seven Pools, though in truth there are more than 20 pools along this stream. The road crosses over 'Ohe'o Gulch between pools 4 and 5.

Hala

Wailua Falls

'Ohe'o Pools

Ke'anae Peninsula

39

'Ohe'o

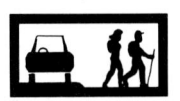

(10.6) Turn left into the 'Ohe'o parking lot and stop by the National Park Ranger Station for brochures telling the story of this special place. You'll notice that this area is surrounded by fields of open land; here again sugar was grown in the early part of the century, and some of the pastures are now used for cattle. But human history at Kipahulu goes back much farther than that; archeological findings show that in pre-Captain Cook times a large population of Hawaiians lived here.

Take the Kuloa loop trail — about half a mile — that starts from the parking lot and crosses grassy slopes down to bluffs overlooking the ocean and the lower pools (see map below). You will see many ancient rock walls and house platforms, reminders of the village that once was here. The trail leads back up along the rushing stream and placid pools, past banks of native plants like beach naupaka and hala, as well as many introduced species. Unless the stream is high the pools are safe for swimming, but do not be tempted to go in the ocean.

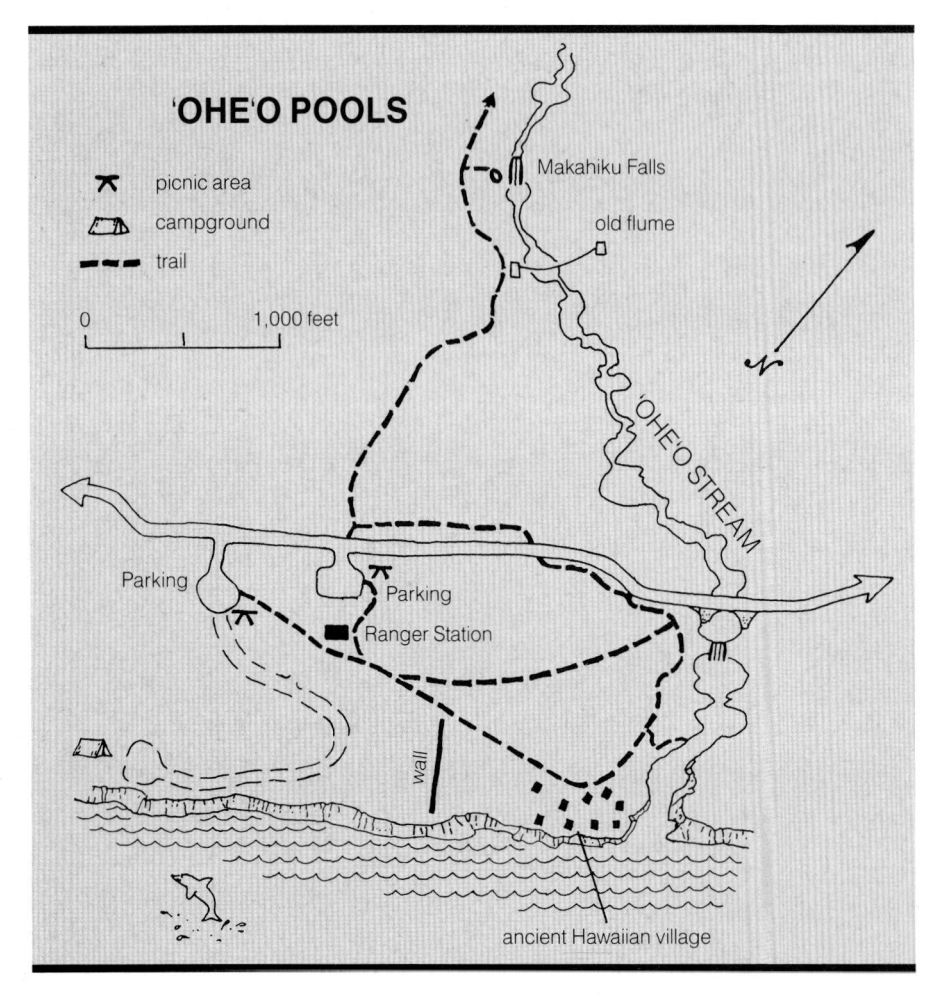

'OHE'O POOLS

- picnic area
- campground
- --- trail

0   1,000 feet

Makahiku Falls
old flume
'OHE'O STREAM
Parking
Parking
Ranger Station
wall
ancient Hawaiian village

Papayas

Though you probably won't see one there is a truly unusual fish that lives in these waters, the 'o'opu, a rare form of goby. These small fish live in fresh water, where their eggs are hatched and washed out to sea. When the young reach sufficient maturity they return to fresh water, swimming up whatever stream is handy. Their remarkable talent is the ability to climb up vertical wet surfaces — like slick rocks beneath waterfalls — using a unique suction cup made of their pelvic fins that enables them to stick to rocks and wiggle their way up.

Kipahulu Valley was added to Haleakala National Park in 1951. Scientists exploring its almost inaccessible upper reaches in 1967 discovered what biological treasures it held. The group, sponsored by the Nature Conservancy, included specialists in such fields as botany, zoology, entomology and plant ecology. All went expecting to find some surprises, but none was prepared for the amazing things they found. Kipahulu proved to be the greatest stronghold of native plants in all of Hawai'i. More than 200 different species of plants were counted, including at least 15 that were previously unknown, and only 20 that had been introduced by man.

Many Kipahulu plants exhibit what botanists call arborescence, or a tendency to evolve into woody, treelike forms — like the species of violet with a strong, woody stem that grows to over eight feet tall. Probably the most spectacular example of arborescence is in the group of Hawaiian lobelias. In home gardens in other parts of the world lobelias are small, colorful but relatively modest ornamentals; Hawai'i has more than 100 species, ranging from two to almost forty feet in height, with curved, tubular flowers. A dozen or more grow in Kipahulu.

The conspicuously curved shape of lobelia blossoms led scientists to an interesting deduction. Since the long curved bills of some of the nectar-sipping honeycreepers exactly echo the shape of the lobelia blossoms, it is believed that they evolved side by side, changing and adapting to each other until bill and flower were a perfect fit.

One of the most exciting discoveries of the exploration came when an ornithologist, moving slowly down a misty trail, caught sight of a bird he did not recognize. He watched it closely through field glasses and, though very familiar with Hawaiian birds, still could not identify it. Back in camp he checked through his reference books and found his mysterious bird on the roster of extinct Hawaiian birds — the Maui nukupu'u, which had not been seen since 1896.

Over the next few days three other extremely rare native birds were seen; the Maui parrotbill — seen only once before in this century, the crested honeycreeper, and the Maui akepa — species making their last stand in Kipahulu Valley.

Studies are continuing in this vast, untouched native koa and 'ohi'a rainforest to find ways to preserve this delicate ecosystem. In this fast-moving world, man seldom finds a way to undo the ecological tragedies that are the side effects of progress. In Kipahulu, it looks as if man — and nature — will have a second chance.

The drive back to Kahului is only 63 miles, but by now you know what the Hana Highway is like; at a safe speed the trip will take about three hours.

HIKING AND CAMPING

Hikers, backpackers, and campers will find some great places to explore on Haleakala and along the Hana Highway. The following selection is arranged by location from the top of the mountain down to the shore.

HALEAKALA CRATER

Hiking within the crater is a visit to another world. It is difficult to describe because it is not like any familiar scene. Some call it a walk on the moon, but the vegetation, unusual though it is, rules that out. Others call it mysterious or strangely beautiful. Take a day or two and see for yourself.

Cabins There are three cabins on the crater floor that can be reserved by lottery (see map on pages 18-19). Apply to Haleakala National Park, P.O. Box 369, Makawao, HI 96768 (telephone 808-572-9306). Since rules change, send for a current cabin information brochure, or ask for one at Park Headquarters. A three-day hike into the crater via the Sliding Sands Trail, overnights at Paliku and Holua Cabins, and out by the Halemau'u Trail is the first-class way to go. The cabins have drinking water, firewood, cooking utensils and bunks. Bring food, a sleeping bag and flashlight. Weather in the crater is extremely variable; it may be hot and sunny for hours, then suddenly change to cold, dense fog or rain. The west end of the crater averages about 45 inches of rainfall per year; the east end more than 100 inches. Good boots, summer and winter hiking clothes, raingear, map, canteen and matches are recommended.

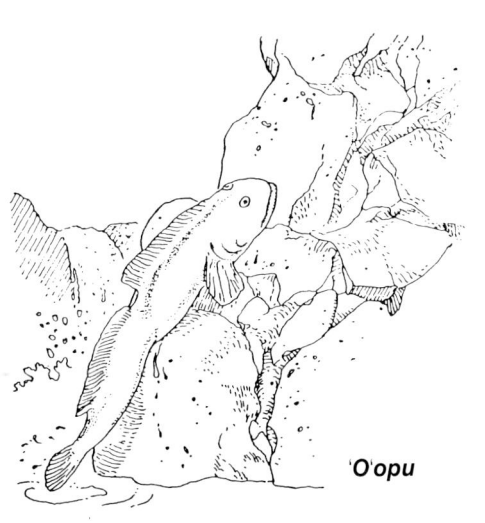

Campgrounds There are two small campgrounds for backpackers near the Holua and Paliku Cabins. Permits must be obtained at Park Headquarters. Drinking water is usually available behind the cabins, but pack in a tent and small cook stove.

Trails Twenty-five miles of trail within the crater lead to or across the sliding sands (volcanic ash and cinders), colorful cinder cones, lava flows, lava tubes, and a "bottomless pit" that is 65 feet deep. Along the way are silverswords, bunch-grass meadows, nene, and the dark-rumped petrel, a rare seabird that nests in the crater cliffs and whose call is like the bark of a young dog.

A strong hiker can descend to the crater floor and back in one day by going down the Sliding Sands Trail and climbing out the Halemau'u Trail (15 miles, 3,000 feet of elevation change); see map on pages 18-19. The short way, down and back on the Halemau'u Trail (starting at 7,990 feet) to the Holua Cabin (6,960 feet), is 8 miles.

Plan ahead so you won't have to hurry. Reserve Paliku and Holua cabins, or check out your backpacking outfit, and spend 3 days hiking the crater. At night the stars look much brighter from this different world. You may even wish to hike

'O'opu

'Ohe'o Stream

Painted bark eucalyptus

Taro

45

out downhill via the Kaupo Gap Trail, but you'll have to arrange to be picked up where the trail meets the road (9 miles and 6,000 feet below Paliku Cabin).

HOSMER GROVE

There is a small campground near the Hosmer Grove parking area (see map page 26). Drinking water, restrooms, grills and firewood are available. This is a good base camp for exploring the summit region.

HANA HIGHWAY

There are several State and County Parks along the road to Hana with hiking trails, picnic tables, restrooms, and campgrounds. These facilities change from time to time so it's best to get specific information from the Maui County Visitors Association, P.O. Box 1738-01B, Kahului, HI 96732 (telephone 808-871-8691). We recommend the following short hiking trail on your way back from Hana if time allows.

Waikamoi Ridge Nature Trail This one-mile loop trail is a great way to experience a jungle rain forest of both native and introduced species. The turnout for the trail is on the upslope side of the Hana Highway in a grove of eucalyptus trees 7 miles west of Ke'anae Arboretum. The path climbs and descends a low ridge through a classic jungle. The upper story is mainly tall eucalyptus trees with huge-leaved monstera vines climbing their trunks. The middle story is hala, palm trees, and some tree ferns; and the lower story a tangle of plants like ginger, ti and philodendron. In a five minute walk from the road you may believe you are in Borneo or the upper Amazon.

KIPAHULU ('OHE'O)

Campground This seaside campground is just down the road from the Kipahulu Ranger Station (see map on page 40). There is no drinking water available, so plan to bring along enough to last your stay.

Makahiku and Waimoku Falls Trail The path to these two beautiful waterfalls begins across the road from the Kipahulu Ranger Station (see map on page 40). The trail to the 185-foot-high Makahiku Falls is a one mile round trip, and to Waimoku Falls is a four mile round trip. The trail ascends through old sugarcane and pasture land that is now growing in with guava, mango and Christmas-berry trees, and thickets of bamboo. The trail can be muddy and slippery; if so, allow nearly as much time hiking down as climbing up. Muddy or not, the trail is verdant and the falls spectacular.

Hawaiian honeycreeper

SUGGESTED READING

General

Beckwith, Martha, HAWAIIAN MYTHOLOGY. Honolulu: University of Hawaii Press, 1970.

Bier, James A., MAP OF MAUI. Honolulu: University of Hawaii Press, 1988.

Chisholm, Craig, HAWAIIAN HIKING TRAILS. Lake Oswego, OR: The Fernglen Press, 1989.

Kepler, Angela Kay, MAUI'S HANA HIGHWAY. Honolulu: Mutual Publishing, 1987.

Kepler, Cameron B., and Angela Kay Kepler, HALEAKALA: A GUIDE TO THE MOUNTAIN. Honolulu: Mutual Publishing, 1988.

Tempski, Armine von, BORN IN PARADISE. Woodbridge, CT: Ox Bow Press, 1985 (original edition, 1940).

Youngblood, Ron, ON THE HANA COAST. Honolulu: Emphasis International Ltd., 1983.

Geology

Decker, Robert, and Barbara Decker, VOLCANOES. New York: W.H. Freeman and Company, 2nd Edition, 1989.

Kyselka, Will, and Ray Lanterman, MAUI: HOW IT CAME TO BE. Honolulu: University of Hawaii Press, 1980.

Macdonald, Gordon, Agatin Abbott, and Frank Peterson, VOLCANOES IN THE SEA. Honolulu: University of Hawaii Press, 1983.

Flora and Fauna

Carlquist, Sherwin, HAWAII: A NATURAL HISTORY. Kauai: Pacific Tropical Botanical Garden, 1980.

Lamoureaux, Charles, TRAILSIDE PLANTS OF HAWAII'S NATIONAL PARKS. Hawaii National Park: Hawaii Natural History Association, 1976.

Merlin, Mark David, HAWAIIAN FOREST PLANTS. Honolulu: The Oriental Publishing Company, 1980.

Nakamura, Adam, and Jan TenBruggencate, WILDLIFE OF HAWAII. Honolulu: The Honolulu Advertiser, 1986.

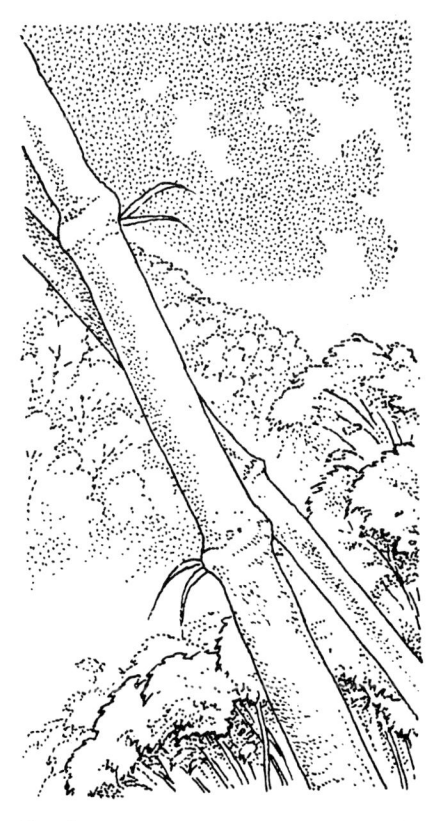

Bamboo

PHOTO CREDITS

All photographs in this road guide were taken by the authors except the following: cover National Park Service, inside cover National Park Service, p.5 National Park Service, p.8 (top) Roger Henneberger, p.10 (top) John Kjargaard, p.10 (bottom) Maile Kjargaard, p.11 Hana Rain Forest Project, p.24 National Park Service, p.34 (next to top) Dwight Hamilton, p.35 (next to top) National Park Service, p.39 (bottom) John Kjargaard.

Makahiku Falls

Torch ginger